CARS STARS Electric guitars

poems by james carter

illustrate
mique moriuchi

WALKER BOOKS
AND SUBSIDIARIES
LONDON · BOSTON · SYDNEY · AUCKLAND

contents

The Shape I'm In

Come and see the shape I'm in

Tall as a tale

Thin as a pin

wide as a smile

Bright — as a tin

Dark as a cave

Curved as a wave

Wild as the rain

strong as a train

I'm *this* and that

I'm here   I'm there

I'm eveRything

&

everywhere!

6

A
garden
shed, a garden
shed, my head is like
a garden shed: it's full of junk and
flower pots, wellie boots and who knows what.

No, really though, my head is crammed
you can't get in, the door is jammed:
with things I've seen, things I've said
things I've done and things I've read.
Plus everything I've thought about
... if I was you – I'd just keep out!!

Rummaging Around

I was rummaging around
inside my head
looking for something
I'd forgotten

and there were so many
things up there —

my Aunty Betty blowing bubbles with soap
all those songs from "The Sound of Music"
the dancing competition at my fifth
    birthday party
and best of all —
the smell of my mum's cooking

so many really interesting things
that I completely forgot
what I was looking for

A Map of Me

What I want
is a map of me –
my future
and my destiny

My who I'll be
my where I'll go
my what I'll do
and need to know

My what I'll see
my what I'll say
my how I'll feel
along the way

But should I wait
for such a thing –
or go and see
what life will bring?

What Makes Me Me

I've been told I've got
Mum's ears
Dad's hair
Gran's chin
and Aunty Emma's
sense of humour

Will they ever want them
back, d'you think?

There's this thing
we could do -
you be me
I'll be you

We'll swap lives
we'll swap clothes
we'll swap shoes
we'll swap homes

Eat my breakfast
I'll eat yours
tease my sister
I'll tease yours

We'll swap mums
we'll swap dads
we'll swap homework
we'll swap cats

Read my diary
I'll read yours
share our secrets...

second thoughts:

NO WAY!!!!

Such a Bad Day

Today was such a bad day
I'd like to dig a huge hole
and bury it deep in the ground

Today was such a bad day
I'd like to wrap it up and feed it
to a very angry and extremely
   hungry shark

Today was such a bad day
I'd like to squeeze it
into a rocket bound for a tiny planet
some 80 billion squillion light
   years away

Then I'd never have to think
   about today
or anything that happened today
   ever ever again

Bauble Blues

oohhh!
it's not much
fun as a Christmas
decoration – I only work
one month a year and then
for the other eleven months
I'm stuffed into a box next
to old goody-two-shoes
the fairy – what a
life, eh?!

Sulky in

I must have been seven
when we went
to St Ives
for a holiday
and I nearly
drowned in the sea

Early afternoon
the tide was out
and I walked
on and on
till I finally got to
the sea

I kept going
till the water
came up
to my middle when suddenly
whoosh
the bottom of the sea
disappeared
and I went
down in the water
down with the bubbles

St Ives

And I kept coming up
kept seeing them all
back on the beach
waving at me

And I kept going down
until one of them
came for me

And I cried
all the way back
to the beach
where everyone laughed
and laughed
at me

And I sulked
for the rest of the day
and I still get sulky
when I think
about it now

Darren

Darren was a dolphin
well, a shiny pink dolphin-shaped
balloon filled with helium gas

We bought him on Bournemouth pier

The first
balloon we
bought that day
was a Buzz Lightyear
but he slipped away by
accident and helpless
we just stood there
w a t c h i n g
h i m g o
u p ,

up, up, up, until he was a tiny speck over the ocean

Darren
had lasted two
whole weeks when
we decided it was time
for him to be reunited with
Buzz in infinity and beyond
So one evening out in the
back garden we just let
Darren go and bit by bit
he drifted up, up, up,
u p ,

above our house

And we
cheered and
c l a p p e d   a n d
whooped "Come on
Darren!" and then he
drifted over, over,
over, over, the
n e x t

door neighbour's house

And we
cheered and
c l a p p e d   a n d
whooped "Come on
Darren!" and then
he drifted down,
down, down,
d o w n ,

into the pub car park

Darren deserved
better than that

Alan's Apple

My mate Alan Greenwood said
you could eat every single bit
   of an apple
if you wanted to

"Even the pips?" I said

"Yup"

"Even the stalk?" I said

"Yup"

"Even the fluffy bit on the
bottom?" I said

"Yup"

And I believed him –
he was good at science
and his Dad was a vet

And I still believe him
but I haven't tried it yet

Rhyming with Orange

People say
nothing rhymes with "orange"
so I'll give it a go:

The peel of an orange
tastes ever so horrange

Oh dear

Where the Words Go

The poem's read, the poet's gone
and yet the words still linger on

And though the listeners cheer and clap
the absent poet won't be back

And as the people leave the hall
the poet's words are with them all

On the train or in the car
and stick with them however far

Their journeys are, beyond the night
and still give pleasure, thrill, excite

And so it goes and so shall it be
for that's the way with poetry

The poem's read, the poet's gone
and yet the words still linger on

their journey are

beyond the night

Favourite Word

Of all the words in all the world
my favourite one is "thingy"
it's everything or nothing at all
plain or fancy, tiny or tall
a do-what-you-like-with-it type of word
something ordinary, something absurd
like "doofer" or "whatsit" or "hoojamaflip"
it may not be trendy or streetwise or hip
but what else will do when a word's on the tip
of your — you know — your whatsit — your doofer
    — oh flip!
and I'm not being silly —
but what was that … thingy?!?!

That Old Magic

I wanted to write a poem

so I tried the old formula:

1 simple idea x 1 tiny bit of imagination +

3 or so drafts = 1 poem

but it didn't work

so I tried it again

and again

and then again

until finally

that old magic crept in

and something really special came along

nice!

TE**A**RDROP

poem
is like
a tear; a drop
of emotion – a tiny
explosion – a silent
commotion – an
act of de-
votion

Inside the Story

I love it when I'm reading a book
and I get to the point where I'm so engrossed
I don't notice the words
on the page any more

I'm actually inside
the world of the story

When I get to that point
you could yell in my ear
you could set off alarm bells
you could pour cold water all over me
you could even set a tiger free in the room
and I wouldn't notice a thing

I'm like that when I'm writing poems too

Hang on —
is that a tiger over there?

An Attempt at the World Record for the Poem That has the Most Long and Boring Title That Just Goes on and on and on for Ever and Ever and Ever and so Much so That it Seems That There Probably Won't Be a Book Big Enough for the Title Let Alone the Poem, But No, Only Joking, Here it is, the Moment You've Been Waiting for, That Little Poem

Little poem
please don't fret
you might grow
much bigger yet

Journey

A poem is a journey

that starts off in your head

a word, a phrase, a thought you've had

or something that you've read

A poem is a journey

not by river, road or rail

or beaten track, or busy street,

or lonely mountain trail

A poem is a journey

to many other worlds

however far your travels are

they're measured out in words

27

A poem is a journey

for which there is no map –

no signposts or directions –

who knows where you'll end up?

A poem is a journey

to lose and find yourself

to go somewhere, to stay right here

to be somebody else

A poem is a journey

to places far and strange

there's only one thing that's for sure –

you won't come back the same

from
a
tiny spring
the river
came
and
wound
its
way
for
days
and
days first
east
then
west
but
always
south
always
down
even
when
it
curled
i
t
f l e s
a
r
o
u n d a b e n
d
but
then
one day
something changed
as it ran so slow but free
for the river grew and the river knew that now it was

THE SEA THE SEA THE SEA THE SEA THE SEA T
SEA THE SEA THE SEA THE SEA THE SEA THE S
THE SEA THE SEA THE SEA THE SEA THE SEA T
SEA THE SEA THE SEA THE SEA THE SEA THE S
THE SEA THE SEA THE SEA THE SEA THE SEA T
SEA THE SE THE SEA TH SEA T E SEA THE S

THE SEA THE SEA THE SEA THE SEA THE SEA
SEA THE SEA THE SEA THE SEA THE SEA THE
THE SEA THE SEA THE SEA THE SEA THE SEA
SEA THE SEA THE SEA THE SEA THE SEA THE
THE SEA THE SEA THE SEA THE SEA THE SEA

F ❋ ❋ r

a bowl of peas

a tea cup

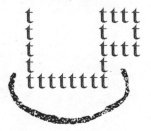

(or a cup of tea)

Kay just loves to watch
the sea

k   c

Letter Poems

bees make honey

```
B           B
B           B
B           B
BBBBBBB     B
B           B
B           B
B           B
```

```
   BBBBBBB
 BB       BB
B           B
B           B
 BB       BB
   BBBBBBB
```

```
B           B
BB          BB
B  B        B B
B    B      B  B
B      B    B B
B           BB
B           B
```

```
BBBBB
B
B
BBBBB
B
B
BBBBB
```

```
B       B
 B     B
  B   B
   B
   B
   B
   B
```

(or honey bees)

6 Things I Want to Know About Noah

1 Did he forget the dinosaurs on purpose?
2 Why did he bother with things like wasps and slugs?
3 Talking about slugs: did he wait for them to slime slowly into the ark – or did another, more nimble creature (perhaps a monkey or a bear) carry them in?
4 Why didn't all the animals eat each other?
5 Did Noah eat any of the animals?
6 Why didn't some of the animals (such as lions and tigers) eat Noah?

Dig It

You know those TV programmes
where they go and dig up places
and find all kinds of interesting things?

Well I'd like one of those TV crews
to come round here
and dig up my garden

I reckon there'd be loads of stuff —

A woolly mammoth's tusk
a Roman soldier's wedding ring
or even a Viking's helmet

But before they started digging
I'd have to remember where I buried
Jaws 1, 2 and 3
the goldfish

Little Dog

Ahh … little dog
Ah … you look all lonely and lost
You lickle diddums

Are you following me now?

Oh … you are a friendly one,
   aren't you, doggy?
Ooh – you're tickling my leg!
Ooh – don't!

Ooh – that hurts
Hey come on –
don't chew my ankle!

Could you get off, please?

Just … just … just … OW!

I'm getting VERY ANGRY NOW

Oi ! ! ! ! !

THAT REALLY HURTS

NOW HOP IT

YOU HORRIBLE

UGLY
MONSTER

There's

There's nothing quite
as yappy as a dog
there's nothing quite as
snappy as a shark
as curly as an eel
as chirpy as a lark
there's nothing quite as
yappy as a dog

There's nothing quite as
hooty as an owl
there's nothing quite as
snooty as a cat
as nippy as a fox
as zippy as a bat
there's nothing quite as
hooty as an owl

Nothing...

There's nothing quite as
growly as a bear

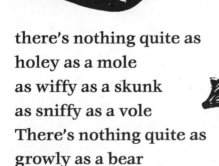

there's nothing quite as
holey as a mole
as wiffy as a skunk
as sniffy as a vole
There's nothing quite as
growly as a bear

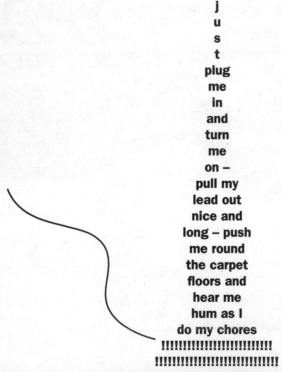

j
u
s
t
plug
me
in
and
turn
me
on –
pull my
lead out
nice and
long – push
me round
the carpet
floors and
hear me
hum as I
do my chores
!!!!!!!!!!!!!!!!!!!!!!!!!!!!
!!!!!!!!!!!!!!!!!!!!!!!!!!!!!!
MMMMMMMMMMMMMMMMMMMMMMMMMMMMMMMMMMMMMMMMMMMMM

Crisp Poem #1

Why should I
give you a crisp?

I know
you've asked nicely

But crisps are crisps
and I'd rather spend
the rest of my pocket money
on buying you
a whole packet
of your own
than give you

  even

   one

    single

    crisp

    from

    this

     packet

     Okay?

Crisp Poem #2

I don't think
there's anything better
than a packet of crisps
and a bottle
of fizz

Nicholas Fulton
thought so too
and invited me over
one Saturday morning
to sit in his dad's shed
with a big bottle
of cream soda
and two huge packets
of salt & vinegars

Once we'd finished
snuffling, slurping
shovelling and guzzling
we couldn't decide
what to do next

So we sat there
burping and hiccuping
in the shed
until lunch-time

Storytimes

Sometimes during storytimes

Timothy sucks his tie

Oliver chews his dinosaur rubber

Rosalyn goes cross-eyed

Yoshi eats her ponytail

Tabitha bites her vest

Isobel wiggles her ears around

Me? What do I like best?

Eating that lovely bubble-gum

Someone left under my desk

Windows

I used to sit and stare out
of windows a lot

My teacher said:
"Stop daydreaming
and get on with your work."

My Mum said:
"Why don't you stop daydreaming
and go and do something?"

In fact
I still daydream every day
and I still stare out of windows —
the kitchen window, the car window,
    train windows —
windows anywhere, anyplace, anytime

By looking out of windows
I listen in to my thoughts —
thoughts that sometimes turn into poems

So why didn't people realize
that I was simply practising
being a poet?

The Girl with the Blue Glasses

We were seven
in the infants together

Every Friday
after games
I asked her
for the same story
over and over again –

The one about
the time her baby brother
went to the loo
in the bath

She giggled through the gap
in her teeth
and I laughed
until I cried
and my tummy hurt
and I couldn't breathe any more

Soon after that
we both went off
to different schools
and I haven't seen her since

What if I bumped into
    her now?
Would I recognize her
and would she still wear those
    blue glasses?

And what would I say to her?
I know:
"What's your brother
up to these days?"

The Worst Thing

For nearly 30 years now
I've been wondering
why I ever agreed to sit next
to Simon Dolan
during our school trip
on that plane to Germany

I knew – I just knew
I should've said "No thank you, Simon"
and left it at that

Here's the thing:
as we boarded the plane
Simon nudged me
and said "Want to sit next to me?"

"Ah..." I said "Umm
Well I suppose..."

"Well that's sorted then," he said
"Bagsy the window seat"

I wasn't that hungry
but Simon tucked into his breakfast
and mine
quite happily

He even asked for seconds

After an hour
Simon said "I get car sick"
and I laughed and said

Ever (Probably)

"Good thing we're on a plane, then"

And he said "I feel car sick now"

And I said "Ah"

And he said "I actually think I'm
going to be sick"

And I said "Go to the loo"

And he said "I actually think I'm
going to be sick right now"

And before I could tell Simon
to go to the loo again
for some very odd reason
that I still don't quite understand
he leant over my lap –
over my favourite
   brown
      flared
         cords
(this was 1972) –
and reminded me
what he'd eaten
for breakfast

On the way back
Simon didn't get the window seat

Mr Baxter the geography teacher
bagsied it instead

Why Did the Chicken Cross the Road?

Why did the chicken cross the road?

Hey, who's askin'? Who'd like to know?
Why should I tell you stuff like that?
You might be some pesky cat
or fox or wolf or hungry bear
so fellow chickens, please beware -
Don't let on when folks ask you -
or everyone will cross roads too!

Electric Guitars

I like electric guitars:
played mellow or moody,
frantic or fast – on CDs
or tapes, at home or in
cars – live in the streets,
at gigs or in bars.
I like
electric
guitars:
played
choppy
like
reggae
or angry
like
rock or
chirpy
like
jazz or
strummy
like
pop or
heavy
like
metal – it
bothers me not.
I like electric guitars:
their strings and their straps
and their wild wammy bars – their
jangling and twanging and funky
wah-wahs – their fuzz boxes,
frets and multi-effects –
pick-ups, machine
heads, mahogany necks
– their plectrums, their wires,
and big amplifiers. I like electric
guitars: played loudly, politely – dully
or brightly – daily or nightly – badly
or nicely. I like electric guitars:
bass, lead and rhythm –
I basically dig 'em –
I like elec t r i c

g u i t a r

I'm sitting on a train and I'm wearing my stereo headphones.

SSSSSSS
BOOM
THUMPITY
TWANG
BIPPITY
KERBOP
BOOOOM

And I'm putting on my favourite tape and pressing "PLAY".

ssssss
BOOM
THUMP
KERRANG
BOOOOP
KERTWANG
BOOOOM

Why's everyone staring at me?!?

Odd *(Body)*......................

Keep an open mind............................

Keep your chin up............................

Turn the other cheek............................

Keep your eyes peeled............................

Pick your feet up............................

Keep your nose clean............................

...............Won't my brain fall out?

...............I'd bump into things,
wouldn't I?

...............Yes, but which one is
"the other"?

...............Ooh ... isn't that painful?

...............And where exactly should
I put them?

...............I already do – and keep
yours out of it!

Cloud Hopping

Some summer evenings
when I couldn't sleep
as it was too light
or too hot
and the neighbours were out
being noisy
in their gardens
I'd take off
in my bed

I'd magic myself
and the bed
small enough
to get through
the open top window
and boof!
off I'd go
up above our house and garden
up above our road
and right up into
the evening sky

When I reached the clouds
I'd park my bed
and I'd wander around

for a while
feeling the wisps
of clouds dissolve
in my hands

Then I'd go
hopping from
   cloud to
      cloud to
         cloud to
            cloud to
               cloud to
                  cloud
until
I'd remember
to get back quickly
or someone might miss me

Then I'd remember
I hadn't been anywhere at all
except in my head

Then I'd still take
absolutely ages
to get to sleep

The Shooting Stars

That night
we went out in the dark
and saw the shooting stars
was one of the best nights ever

It was as if someone
was throwing paint
across the universe

The stars just kept coming
and we "oohed" and "aahed"
like on bonfire night

And it didn't matter
they weren't real stars —
just bits of dust on fire
burning up in the atmosphere

And we stayed out there for ages
standing on this tiny planet
staring up at the vast cosmos

And I shivered
with the thrill
of it all

The Dark

Why are we so afraid of the dark?
It doesn't bite and doesn't bark
or chase old ladies round the park
or steal your sweeties for a lark

And though it might not let you see
it lets you have some privacy
and gives you time to go to sleep —
provides a place to hide or weep

It cannot help but be around
when beastly things make beastly sounds
or back doors slam and windows creak
or cats have fights and voices shriek

The dark is cosy, still and calm
and never does you any harm
in the loft, below the sink
it's somewhere nice and quiet to think

Deep in cupboards, pockets too
it's always lurking out of view
why won't it come out till it's night?
perhaps the dark's afraid of light

Haiku Triptych

A tiny green frog
sits upon a lily pad
idly moongazing

Nearby a brown moth
on finding a nice streetlight
boogies all night long

Inside a small boy
hypnotized by the TV
bathes in its blue haze

Night Car Journey

I wake up
sitting in the back seat
not quite sure
if it's real or a dream

and I look up
out through the darkness
out through the silence
to an infinite sky

and the moon bobs
in and out of treetops
turning the world
a ghostly blue

and my eyes
are heavy now
my eyes
are heavy now
my

The Life

The world turned round
the sun came up
then people yawned
and drank a cup

Of tea and went
about their day
busy, busy
on their way

Clouds were cloudy
dogs chased tails
cars had jams
shops had sales

Nurses cared
mothers loved
scarecrows scared
lovers hugged

Singers sang
dolphins swam
itches itched
mobiles rang

# of a Day

Babies cried
teardrops dried
teachers sighed
pupils tried

Queues queued up
socks fell down
shows went on
friends came round

Prayers were said
stairs were steep
books were read
thoughts were deep

Sky was sky
and sea was sea
and you were you
and I was me

And the sun went down
and the moon shone bright
and that was the life of a day
– goodnight!

For
Sarah, Lauren and Madeleine
with all my love
J. C.

Aki
M. M.

The author thanks Jacqueline Wilson, Annie Eaton,
Brian Moses, Paul Harrison, Caroline Royds,
Beth Aves, Patrick Insole, Helen Fairlie
and of course Mique Moriuchi

First published 2002 by
Walker Books Ltd
87 Vauxhall Walk
London SE11 5HJ

This edition published 2007
2 4 6 8 10 9 7 5 3 1

Text © 2002 James Carter
Illustrations © 2002 Mique Moriuchi

The moral rights of the author and illustrator
have been asserted.

This book has been typeset in Franklin Gothic,
Jacobs-Rubberstamp and Veljovik

Printed and bound in Great Britain by
Creative Print and Design (Wales)

ISBN 978-1-4063-1209-6

www.walkerbooks.co.uk